Sikh Festivals
Through the Year

Anita Ganeri

FRANKLIN WATTS
LONDON • SYDNEY

© 2003 Franklin Watts

First published in Great Britain by
Franklin Watts
96 Leonard Street
LONDON EC2A 4XD

Franklin Watts Australia
45–51 Huntley Street
Alexandria
NSW 2015

ISBN: 0 7496 4800 7
A CIP catalogue record for this book
is available from the British Library

Printed in Hong Kong, China

Editor: Kate Banham
Art Direction: Jonathan Hair
Educational Consultant: Alan Brown
Faith Consultant: Rajinder Singh Panesar, Bradford Interfaith Centre

Designer: Joelle Wheelwright
Map (p7): Aziz Khan
Picture Research: Diana Morris

Acknowledgements
The publishers would like to thank the following for permission to
reproduce photographs in this book:
Gordon Clements/Axiom: 25tr; B.Dhanjal/Trip: 22tr; Dinodia Photo Library: 26b;
Paul Doyle/Photofusion: 13t, 20t; Paul Gapper/World Religions Photo Library: 26t;
Arvind Garg/Corbis: 15tl; Prem Kapoor/World Religions Photo Library: 19b;
Christine Osborne/World Religions Photo Library: front cover, 10bl, 17t, 23t, 24t;
H. Rogers/Trip: 6c, 10tr,11c,16t,18r, 21t, 22bl, 25bl, 27t; Trip: 8b, 14t.

Whilst every attempt has been made to clear copyright, should there be any inadvertent
omission please apply in the first instance to the publisher regarding rectification.

Contents

Introduction —————————————————— 6

The Sikh Gurus ——————————————— 8

Guru Nanak's Birthday —————————— 10

Birthday Celebrations ————————— 12

Guru Tegh Bahadur —————————— 14

Guru Gobind Singh's Birthday ———— 16

Hola Mohalla ————————————— 18

Baisakhi ———————————————— 20

Celebrating Baisakhi ————————— 22

Guru Arjan Dev ——————————— 24

Divali ————————————————— 26

Festival Calendar —————————— 28

Glossary ——————————————— 29

Further Resources ————————— 30

Index ———————————————— 30

Words printed in **bold** are explained in the glossary.

Introduction

Sikhs are people who follow the religion of Sikhism. It began about 500 years ago in Punjab, north-west India. At that time, **Hinduism** and **Islam** were the main religions in India. But they were deeply divided, and many people felt left out. A holy man, Nanak, introduced the new religion of Sikhism which taught tolerance and equality. He became the first Sikh **Guru**, or teacher. Today, there are about 14 million Sikhs. Most still live in India.

The Golden Temple in Amritsar, India, is the centre of the Sikh faith.

Festival dates

Sikh festivals are traditionally based on the ancient Hindu lunar calendar. The lunar year is shorter than the solar year on which the everyday Western calendar is based. To bring the two calendars into line, an extra month is added every few years. In 1999, a new Sikh calendar was introduced, called *Nanakshahi*, or 'Royal Nanak'. It dates from 1469, the year of Guru Nanak's birth. (See page 28 for the names of the Hindu months and the names of the *Nanakshahi* months.) But the vast majority of Sikhs still use the Hindu lunar calendar to work out the timings of festivals.

Sikh beliefs

Sikhs believe that there is only one God. They hope to grow closer to God by remembering God in everything they do, working hard, living honestly and caring for others. The ideal of looking after others, without thought of your own reward, is very important for Sikhs. It is called *sewa*, or service. Another key belief is that everyone – men and women, rich and poor – is equal in God's eyes. All religions lead to the same God, and should all be tolerated.

How Sikhs worship

A *Gurdwara* is a building where Sikhs meet for worship and to learn more about their faith. The word *Gurdwara* means 'gateway to the Guru'. Any building can be a *Gurdwara*, as long as it contains a copy of the **Guru Granth Sahib**, the Sikhs' holy book. In the *Gurdwara*, Sikhs listen to readings from the holy book, sing **shabads**, or hymns, and say prayers. Afterwards, they share a meal, called **langar**. Everyone takes turns to cook and serve langar, to show that everyone is equal.

Sikhs worshipping in a Gurdwara, in front of the Guru Granth Sahib.

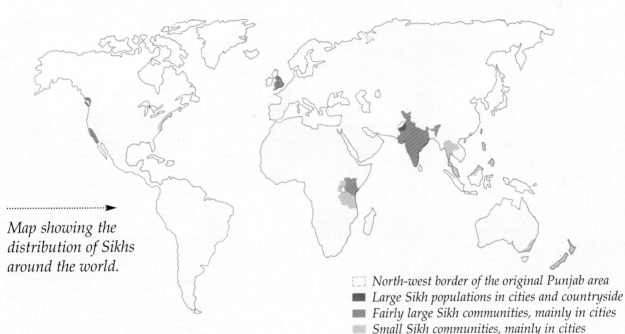

Map showing the distribution of Sikhs around the world.

☐ *North-west border of the original Punjab area*
■ *Large Sikh populations in cities and countryside*
▨ *Fairly large Sikh communities, mainly in cities*
▧ *Small Sikh communities, mainly in cities*

Sikh festivals

There are two kinds of Sikh festivals – *gurpurbs* and *jore melas*. 'Gurpurb' means 'Guru's day'. These festivals remember key times in the lives of the ten Sikh Gurus, such as their birthdays and deaths. The word 'jore' means a gathering, and 'mela' means a fair. These festivals celebrate other great events from Sikh history. They are less serious occasions than *gurpurbs*, with funfair rides, stalls and dancing. Festivals are important for reminding Sikhs of their history and inspiring them to live good lives.

The Sikh Gurus

Guru Nanak was the first Sikh Guru. Before he died, he chose one of his followers to be Guru after him. For the next 170 years, Sikh beliefs were passed down through a chain of Gurus. In the Punjabi language, the word 'Guru' means a teacher inspired by God. There are ten human Gurus and the Guru Granth Sahib (see right). The Gurus teach Sikhs how to grow closer to God.

A painting showing the Sikh Gurus.

The Ten Gurus

This list gives the names of the ten Sikh Gurus, with the dates of their births and deaths, and some of their main achievements.

1   **Guru Nanak (1469–1539)** was the first Guru of the Sikh religion. He taught the basic Sikh beliefs and established many Sikh customs, such as *langar*.

2   **Guru Angad Dev (1504–1552)** finalised *Gurmukhi*, the script in which the Guru Granth Sahib is written. The word '*Gurmukhi*' means 'from the Guru's mouth'.

3   **Guru Amar Das (1479–1574)** encouraged the Sikhs to gather together twice a year to celebrate the festivals of *Baisakhi* and *Divali*.

4   **Guru Ram Das (1534–1581)** founded the city of Amritsar in Punjab, the centre of the Sikh faith. He also composed the *Lavan*, the Sikh wedding hymn.

5   **Guru Arjan Dev (1563–1606)** built the Harimandir (Golden Temple) in Amritsar (see page 6). He collected the Sikh sacred writings together to form the Guru Granth Sahib.

6   **Guru Hargobind (1595–1644)** encouraged the Sikhs to fight for what they believed in. He wore two swords which stood for spiritual and worldly power.

7   **Guru Har Rai (1630–1661)** helped to spread the Sikh religion. He also set up hospitals which gave free medicines and treatment to everyone who needed it.

8   **Guru Har Krishan (1656–1664)** was only five when he became Guru. He is remembered for caring for the sick until he died of smallpox at the age of eight.

9   **Guru Tegh Bahadur (1621–1675)** helped the Hindus to stand up to the Muslim Mughal emperor. The emperor later had him arrested and killed.

10 **Guru Gobind Singh (1666–1708)** was the last of the human Gurus. At the festival of *Baisakhi* in 1699 he set up the **Khalsa**, the Sikh community.

A Sikh worshipper reading from the Guru Granth Sahib.

Guru Granth Sahib

When Guru Gobind Singh was close to death, he did not name a person to succeed him as Guru. In future, he told the Sikhs, their Guru would be the Guru Granth Sahib, their holy book. The Guru Granth Sahib is made up of hymns, mostly composed by the Gurus. Sikhs believe that it is the word of God and treat it with the greatest respect.

Mool Mantar

The Mool Mantar prayer begins the Guru Granth Sahib. It was composed by Guru Nanak and sums up Sikh beliefs about God:

'There is only one God
Whose name is Truth
God the creator
Is without fear
Is without hate
Is timeless and without shape
Is beyond death, the enlightened one
And is understood through God's grace.'

Guru Nanak's Birthday

In November, Sikhs all over the world remember the birthday of Guru Nanak, the first Sikh Guru. This is one of the most important times in the Sikh calendar. You can read about how Sikhs celebrate this festival on pages 12–13.

A painting of Guru Nanak, the first Sikh Guru and teacher of the Sikh religion.

A **Gurdwara** *built in honour of Guru Nanak in his birthplace near Lahore in Pakistan.*

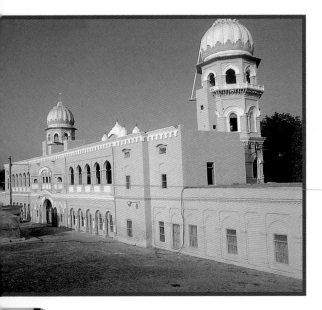

Guru Nanak's birth

Guru Nanak was born in 1469 in the village of Talwandi, south-west of Lahore (now in Pakistan). His family were Hindus. From an early age, Nanak was deeply religious and, according to Sikh stories, several events from his childhood marked him out as special. Once, he fell asleep while looking after some cattle, which wandered off and trampled a neighbour's crop of wheat. The neighbour was very angry but Nanak told him not to worry. When the neighbour looked at his field again, the crop was better than ever.

Vision of God

When Nanak was about 30 years old, he went down to the river to bathe as usual, but did not come back home. His friends and family thought that he must have drowned. But three days later, Nanak returned. He said that he had been taken up into heaven, and had seen God. God told Nanak to teach people how to live good and truthful lives. Nanak told his friends, 'I know now that God is neither Hindu nor Muslim, so the path I shall follow is neither Hindu nor Muslim, but God's.' From that time, Nanak became known as 'Guru'.

A Hymn by Guru Nanak

'I was an out of work minstrel.
God gave me work.
God gave me the order,
"Sing my praise night and day".
God summoned the minstrel
to the divine court.
He bestowed on me the robe of
honouring God and singing
His divine praises.'

A painting of Guru Nanak (with halo) and his friend, Mardana (seated).

Travels and teachings

Guru Nanak gave up his job and possessions, and became a wandering teacher. He taught that there is one God, and that everyone is equal in God's eyes. Guru Nanak often used poetry to explain these teachings. His verses were set to music by his faithful travelling companion, the Muslim musician, Mardana.

When Guru Nanak was an old man, he settled in the village of Kartarpur in the Punjab. People came from far and wide to learn from him. Just before he died, Guru Nanak chose Guru Angad Dev to be his successor.

Birthday Celebrations

Every *gurpurb* festival (in honour of a Guru's birthday) is celebrated in a similar way, with a reading of the Guru Granth Sahib, services in the *Gurdwara* and street processions.

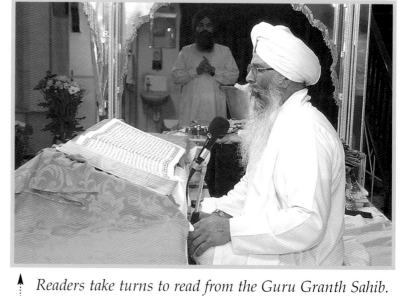

Readers take turns to read from the Guru Granth Sahib.

Akhand Path

The most important part of a *gurpurb* is a reading of the Guru Granth Sahib from beginning to end. This is called an **Akhand Path** which means 'unbroken recitation'. An *Akhand Path* is held in the *Gurdwara*, and takes about 48 hours. It is timed to end early on the morning of the day of the festival. Readers work in teams, and no one reads for more than two hours at a time because the words must be clear. A reserve reader is always ready to take over if someone falls ill.

Gurdwara service

During the *Akhand Path*, many Sikhs drop into the *Gurdwara* to listen for a while, then go home again. After the reading is completed, a service is held. There are talks about the meaning of the *gurpurb*, and hymns in praise of the Guru. At the end of every Sikh service, people share a sweet mixture, called **karah parshad** (see page 17). The act of sharing is a way of showing that everyone is equal. Afterwards, *langar* is served.

A meal is served after every Sikh service.

↑ *Sikhs dressed as the* Panj Piare.

Street processions

In India, and in other countries with large Sikh communities, there are processions through the streets to celebrate a *gurpurb*. The procession is led by five devout Sikh men who represent the **Panj Piare**, or five beloved ones, who were the first members of the *Khalsa*, or Sikh community (see pages 20–21). They wear orange or yellow robes and turbans, as the *Panj Piare* wore. Behind them comes a beautifully decorated float which carries the Guru Granth Sahib. The congregation follow the float, singing hymns written by the Gurus and other holy men. People watching the procession are often given sweets or drinks as a way of joining in.

A Birthday Hymn

These lines are from the most popular shabad *sung at Guru Nanak's birthday.*
It is by a Sikh writer, called Bhai Gurdas.

'The merciful Lord heard the cries of humanity
And sent Guru Nanak to this earth.
He prayed to God in utter humility and gave the nectar
of God's name to his followers.
In the dreadful Dark Age,
Guru Nanak sang God's praise.
The Guru established the Sikh religion
and brought all people together.
He treated prince and pauper alike and his followers
learned to bow in humility to each other.
He performed this unique act
to teach humility to his followers.
Baba Nanak liberated people from the
Dark Age and taught them God's true name.
Guru Nanak came to this world to save humankind.'

Guru Tegh Bahadur

Another *gurpurb* takes place in November to mark the death of the ninth Guru, Guru Tegh Bahadur. Sikhs remember how, in 1675, Guru Tegh Bahadur gave up his life for the right to practise his own religion freely. Sikhs believe that he is an example for all religions to follow. A person who dies for his or her faith is called a martyr, and their death is called martyrdom.

·····················➤

A painting of Guru Tegh Bahadur, whose death is marked in November.

The Guru dies for his faith

In Guru Tegh Bahadur's time, India was ruled by the Mughal Emperor Aurangzeb who was a devout Muslim. Aurangzeb wanted to force all Hindus and Sikhs to become Muslims. Many Hindus were killed because they refused to give up their faith. A group of Hindu holy men came to ask Guru Tegh Bahadur for his help. They knew that he taught that everyone had the right to follow their own way of life. The Guru told the holy men to send a message to the emperor. The message said that if the emperor could persuade Guru Tegh Bahadur to convert to Islam, all Hindus would follow his example.

The emperor was delighted. He called the Guru to Delhi and offered him palaces, and other riches if he became a Muslim. But the Guru refused. Furious, the emperor threatened him with torture. But still the Guru would not give up his faith. So the emperor had him tortured and his head cut off.

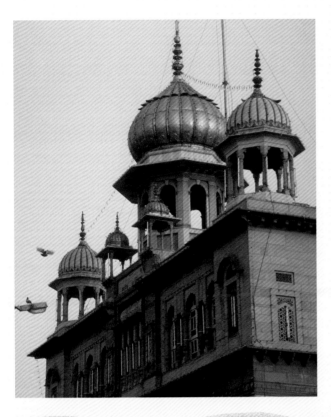

Remembering the Guru

Like most *gurpurbs*, Guru Tegh Bahadur's death is remembered by holding an *Akhand Path*, saying prayers, singing hymns and with street processions. This *gurpurb* is especially important in Delhi, the capital of India. This is where the Guru was put to death. A beautiful *Gurdwara* called the Sis Ganj Sahib Gurdwara has been built on the site of his execution.

←....................

The Sis Ganj Sahib Gurdwara in Delhi, India, the site of Guru Tegh Bahadur's martyrdom.

A *romalla*

When the Guru Granth Sahib is not being read, it is covered with a beautifully decorated cloth, called a *romalla*. On special occasions, such as the completion of an *Akhand Path*, Sikhs make an offering of a *romalla* in the *Gurdwara*.

To make a romalla:

1. Cut a piece of brightly coloured cloth, about 1 metre by 1.25 metres. Turn over the edges, and sew or stick the hems down.

2. Sew or stick a length of gold braid around the edges of the cloth.

3. Decorate the cloth using fabric pens or paints. Draw geometric

patterns, flowers and leaves, and Sikh symbols, such as the 'Ik Onkar' (right) which means 'There is only one God'.

Guru Gobind Singh's Birthday

The birthday of Guru Gobind Singh, the tenth Sikh Guru, falls in January. It is celebrated by Sikhs all over the world. Special celebrations take place in Patna, India, where Guru Gobind Singh was born.

A painting of the tenth Sikh Guru, Guru Gobind Singh.

A *Shabad* by Guru Gobind Singh

'Grant me this boon
O God, from Thy greatness.
May I never refrain
From righteous acts.
May I fight without fear
All foes in life's battle,
With confident courage
Claiming the victory!
May Thy glory be
Ever in my mind,
And my highest ambition be
Singing Thy praises.
When this mortal life
Reaches its end,
May I die fighting
With limitless courage!'

The life of Guru Gobind Singh

Guru Gobind Singh was born in 1666. He became Guru at the age of nine, after the death of his father, Guru Tegh Bahadur (see pages 14–15). Guru Gobind Singh was a brilliant scholar, a brave warrior, and had a kind and generous nature. He had to fight many battles to protect the Sikhs and their religious freedom. In 1699, at the festival of Baisakhi, he began the *Khalsa*, or Sikh community (see pages 20–21). Guru Gobind Singh did not name a human Guru to lead the Sikhs after him. Just before he died in 1708, he told the Sikhs to look to the Guru Granth Sahib for their spiritual guidance.

Celebrations

Guru Gobind Singh's birthday is marked with a *gurpurb*, very similar to that held on Guru Nanak's birthday. In India, the festival takes place on the day itself. In other countries, such as Britain, it is usually celebrated on the nearest Sunday. In Britain, the roads are sealed off so that a procession of the *Panj Piare* and the Guru Granth Sahib can take place. The procession passes by the local *Gurdwaras*, which are decorated with banners and flowers.

Celebrations for Guru Gobind Singh's birthday in London.

Karah parshad

Karah parshad is a sweet mixture shared out at the end of Sikh services. To make *karah parshad*, you will need:

1 cup of sugar
1 cup of unsalted butter
1 cup of semolina
Half a cup of water

1. Melt the butter in a saucepan over a low heat.

2. Add the semolina and cook for a few minutes until it is golden brown.

3. Mix in the sugar and the water, and stir until thick.

4. Leave to cool, then share with your friends.

Hola Mohalla

The festival of *Hola Mohalla*, which means 'the place to attack', is celebrated in February or March at about the same time as the great Hindu spring festival of *Holi*. *Hola Mohalla* is a *jore mela*, a colourful, lively time in the Sikh calendar.

A Sikh dressed as a Nihang, or Sikh warrior. Groups of Nihangs travel through the Punjab, taking part in festivals such as Hola Mohalla.

How *Hola Mohalla* began

Hola Mohalla was begun in 1680 in the town of Anandapur, northern India, by Guru Gobind Singh, the tenth Sikh Guru. He felt that the Hindu festival of *Holi* had become too frivolous, and decided that the Sikhs should have their own festival on the day after *Holi*. He summoned the Sikhs together to practise the military skills they needed to defend their faith against the Mughal rulers. They brought their weapons, fought mock battles and took part in military drills and parades, as if they were on a real battlefield. At the end, Guru Gobind Singh led an attack on a model castle.

Celebrating *Hola Mohalla*

Today, *Hola Mohalla* is mainly celebrated in Anandapur, where it began. Thousands of Sikhs gather there to take part in the festival. After a morning service in the *Gurdwara*, there are displays of martial arts and sporting contests, such as swordsmanship, archery, wrestling matches and horse-riding. These are followed by music and poetry competitions. Hymn singing and religious talks take place in the presence of the Guru Granth Sahib. There is also a great parade, led by Sikhs dressed as the *Panj Piare*, carrying the flags of the local *Gurdwaras*. *Hola Mohalla* is also marked by some Sikhs in Britain, the USA and Canada.

A demonstration of martial arts at Hola Mohalla.

Kabaddi

Local sporting competitions often take place around the time of *Hola Mohalla*. *Kabaddi* is an Indian game that is also played by Sikhs living in Britain. The word *Kabaddi* literally means dividing an area into two halves.

There are two teams of players. The aim of the game is for one player to break through a row of members of the other team, as they try to touch him or wrestle him to the ground. At the same time, he has to take a deep breath and repeat '*Kabaddi*' for as long as he can before taking another breath. As soon as he runs out of breath and takes another he has to stop.

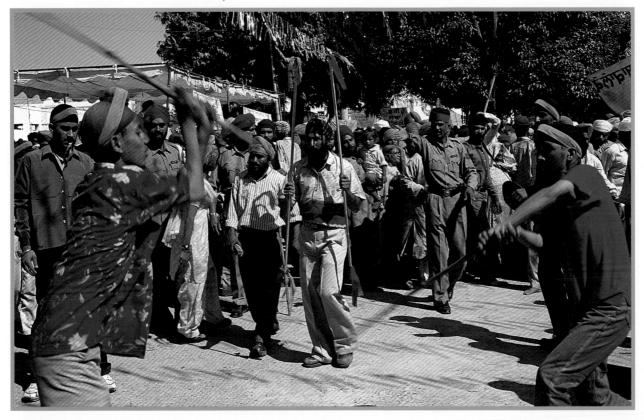

Baisakhi

On 13 or 14 April, Sikhs celebrate the festival of *Baisakhi*. At this time, they remember a very important event in Sikh history – the founding of the *Khalsa*, or Sikh community, by Guru Gobind Singh, the tenth Sikh Guru. The word *Baisakhi* comes from the name of the month in which the festival falls (see page 28). In India, *Baisakhi* also marks the start of the New Year for Sikhs, when the winter wheat crop was harvested.

Happy Baisakhi!

The Story of *Baisakhi*

On *Baisakhi* in 1699, Guru Gobind Singh called the Sikhs together. About 20,000 Sikhs came to Anandapur, where the Guru lived. With his sword in his hand, Guru Gobind Singh asked if any of them were willing to die for their faith. Nobody replied. The Guru asked a second time. Still, nobody replied. When he asked a third time, a man called Darya Ram stepped forward. The Guru took him to his tent and returned minutes later, his sword dripping with blood. The crowd was horrified. The Guru asked for another Sikh and led him into his tent. He repeated his question three more times, and three more brave men came forward.

The *Panj Piare*

Then, an amazing thing happened. Guru Gobind Singh led the five men out of his tent, alive and unharmed. Like the Guru, they were dressed in bright yellow robes, blue sashes and yellow turbans. The Guru explained to the crowd that these five men had proved their courage by being ready to die for their faith. From now on, they would be called the *Panj Piare* – the five beloved ones. They were the first members of the *Khalsa*, the new community of Sikhs.

The Guru prepared **amrit**, a special mixture of sugar and water for the *Panj Piare* to drink. Then the Guru drank *amrit* from the same bowl. This showed that everyone was equal in God's eyes. Afterwards, many other Sikhs came forward to join the *Khalsa*.

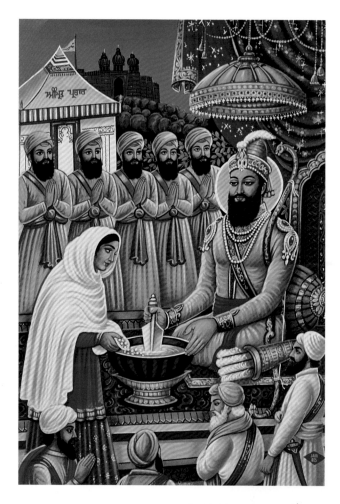

A painting of Guru Gobind Singh and the Panj Piare *at the founding of the* Khalsa.

Five Ks

At *Baisakhi*, Guru Gobind Singh asked all Sikhs who joined the *Khalsa* to wear five items. These are known as the Five Ks because they all begin with the letter 'K' in the Punjabi language:

1. *Kesh* – uncut hair. This shows obedience and devotion to God. Men keep their hair wrapped in a turban.

2. *Kangha* – a small wooden comb. This keeps long hair tidy. It reminds Sikhs of the importance of order and honesty.

3. *Kara* – a steel bracelet worn on the right wrist. Its circular shape shows unity with God and the *Khalsa*.

4. *Kirpan* – a small ceremonial sword. This symbolises courage and willingness to fight for justice.

5. *Kachera* – a special pair of shorts, worn as underwear. These were originally worn in battle.

Celebrating Baisakhi

Baisakhi is celebrated by Sikhs all over the world. It is a *jore mela*, a time for Sikhs to come together and show their commitment to their faith. There are services in the *Gurdwara* with prayers, hymns and talks, and an *Akhand Path* is held. Some places have street processions led by the *Panj Piare*.

A street procession at Baisakhi.

Joining the *Khalsa*

Baisakhi is a time when many young Sikhs join the *Khalsa* at a special *amrit* ceremony held in the *Gurdwara*. It is led by five people, representing the *Panj Piare*. The people who are to enter the *Khalsa* bathe and put on the Five Ks. During the ceremony, they kneel and receive *amrit* in their cupped hands. They drink it five times. It is also sprinkled on their eyes and hair. They are then members of the *Khalsa*, and promise to follow the teachings of the Gurus.

Stirring the amrit *mixture for the amrit ceremony.*

The *Nishan Sahib* flag

The Sikh flag flies outside every *Gurdwara*. At *Baisakhi*, the flagpole is taken down and cleaned, and the flag and flagpole coverings are replaced. The flag is called the **Nishan Sahib**, which means 'respected flag'. It is triangular and made from yellow cloth, with a black *khanda* symbol in the centre. The *khanda* is made up of a double-edged sword which stands for God's power. Around it is a circle to show that God has no beginning nor end. The two crossed swords on the outside symbolise earthly and spiritual power. The *Nishan Sahib* was given to the Sikhs by the sixth Guru, Hargobind, to lead them in battle.

.......................➤

Changing the Nishan Sahib *flag at* Baisakhi.

New names

When Sikhs join the *Khalsa*, they are given new names as instructed by Guru Gobind Singh. He wanted Sikhs to share a name to show that they belonged to the same family. Men take the name '*Singh*' which means lion and represents courage. Women take the name '*Kaur*' which means princess to show their important status.

A *Nishan Sahib* flag

You can make this flag any size you like.

1. Cut out a triangle of yellow cloth.
2. Cut out a *khanda* symbol from black cloth and stick or sew it on the triangle. It may be easier to make the symbol in pieces – the double-edged sword, the circle and the two swords – then put it all together.
3. Fold the side of the triangle around a piece of dowelling, and glue it in place.
4. Make another *khanda* symbol from card covered in cooking foil. Glue this to the top of the flagpole.

.......................➤

A small khanda *symbol made from card and foil.*

Guru Arjan Dev

In June, a *gurpurb* is held which marks the death of Guru Arjan Dev, the fifth Sikh Guru, in 1606. On this day, Sikhs remember how Guru Arjan Dev was put to death by the Mughal emperor, Jahangir, because he refused to give up his beliefs. Sikhs say that Guru Arjan Dev was the first Sikh martyr.

A painting of Guru Arjan Dev, who was put to death for standing by his religious beliefs.

Story of Guru Arjan Dev

Guru Arjan Dev became Guru in 1581 when he was 18 years old. At that time, India was ruled by Emperor Akbar who was friendly towards the Sikhs. But when Akbar died, his son, Jahangir, a devout Muslim, became emperor instead. Jahangir did not like the Sikh religion because he thought that it was becoming too popular. When Jahangir found out that his rebellious son, Prince Khusro, had visited the Guru, he was furious. He believed that the Guru was plotting against him and ordered him to pay a huge fine. He also told him to change the words of the Guru Granth Sahib. Guru Arjan Dev refused to alter the holy book and said that he only had money for the poor and needy.

A terrible fate

Hearing this, Jahangir had the Guru arrested and locked up in prison in Lahore. Then he had the Guru tortured. For three days, the Guru was locked in a cell without food or water, even though it was summer and baking hot. Over the next few days, he was put in a barrel of boiling water, had burning sand poured over him, and was made to sit on a red-hot iron plate. Even then, the Guru would not give in, or complain about fate. Finally, he was pushed into the River Ravi where he drowned.

The River Ravi, where Guru Arjan Dev drowned.

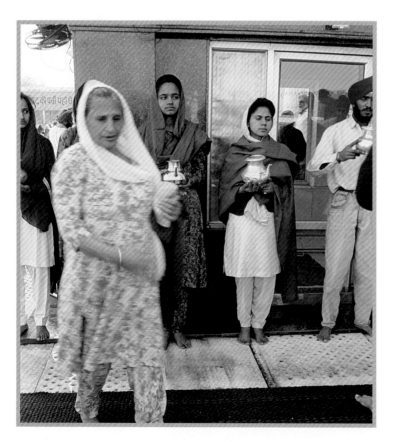

Sikhs serving water to passers-by to mark Guru Arjan Dev's death.

Cool drinks

Sikhs mark Guru Arjan's death by listening to stories about his life and death. It is also the custom to set up roadside stalls, serving free, cold drinks to passers-by. This reminds Sikhs of the terrible thirst Guru Arjan Dev suffered as he was being tortured. The drinks also show that Sikhs have no bad feelings towards anyone and that no one should suffer as the Guru did. Looking after others is very important for Sikhs. Handing out drinks is a way of serving people and of serving God.

Divali

The third *jore mela* in the Sikh calendar is *Divali*, the festival of lights. It is celebrated in October or November by Sikhs all around the world. At *Divali*, Sikhs remember how the sixth Guru, Guru Hargobind, returned home to Amritsar after his release from prison.

Sikhs in London lighting candles for Divali.

The story of *Divali*

After Guru Arjan Dev's death, the Sikhs realised that they would have to fight to defend their faith. Guru Arjan Dev's son and successor, Guru Hargobind, began to train an army. This worried Emperor Jahangir. To find out more about it, he invited the Guru on a hunting trip. On this trip, Guru Hargobind saved the Emperor's life when a tiger leapt out and attacked him. After this, the two men became friends. Then the emperor fell ill. He was told that he would only recover if a holy man prayed for his good health. So he asked the Guru to go to Gwalior Fort to pray for him. In the fort, Guru Hargobind was treated very well. But the fort was also a prison and the 52 Hindu princes kept captive there were not so lucky. They had only rags to wear and very little to eat. The Guru tried to help them in any way he could.

Hindu *Divali*

Divali is one of the most important festivals of the year for Hindus. But it is celebrated by Hindus for a different reason. There are many stories associated with the Hindu *Divali* festival. One story tells of how the god, Rama, and his wife, Sita, returned from exile to be crowned king and queen. At *Divali*, Hindus light *diva* lamps to guide Rama and Sita home.

The Guru's cloak

Jahangir recovered from his illness and told the Guru that he was free to go. But the Guru refused to leave the fort unless the Hindu princes were also freed. Jahangir was horrified. He told the Guru that he could take as many princes as could hold on to his cloak when he left the fort. The emperor knew that the gateway was very narrow. He thought that the Guru would only be able to take four or five princes with him, but no more. But the Guru was even more clever. He had a cloak made, with 52 long silk tassels, one for each of the princes. Then he walked out of the fort, taking all the princes with him.

·····························▶

A painting of Guru Hargobind leading the Hindu princes out of Gwalior Fort.

The Golden Temple in Amritsar at Divali. ↓

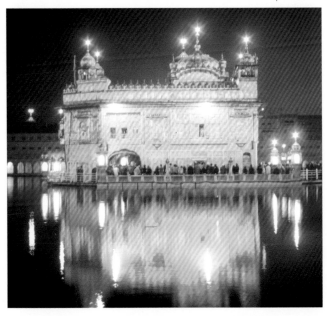

Celebrating Divali

When Guru Hargobind returned home to Amritsar after his release, the Sikhs decorated the Harimandir (Golden Temple) with lights to welcome him. Every year, at Divali, the whole of the Golden Temple is again illuminated to remember this happy event. There are also firework displays. Many Sikhs light their homes with candles, or small clay lamps, called *divas*, to welcome Guru Hargobind home. They also go to services in the *Gurdwara*, which are specially decorated for the occasion.

Festival Calendar

Month	Festival
October/November	Guru Nanak's birthday
November/December	Guru Tegh Bahadur's martyrdom
December/January	Guru Gobind Singh's birthday
February/March	*Hola Mohalla*
13/14 April	*Baisakhi*
June	Guru Arjan Dev's martyrdom
October/November	*Divali*

Sikh months

In the Hindu lunar calendar, the months are:

Magha	(January/February)
Phalguna	(February/March)
Chaitra	(March/April)
Vaisakha	(April/May)
Jyeshtha	(May/June)
Ashadha	(June/July)
Shravana	(July/August)
Badra	(August/September)
Ashvina	(September/October)
Karttika	(October/November)
Margashirsha	(November/December)
Pausha	(December/January)

In the *Nanakshahi* calendar, the months are:

Katik	(October/November)
Maghar	(November/December)
Poh	(December/January)
Magh	(January/February)
Phagan	(February/March)
Chet	(March/April)
Vaisakh	(April/May)
Jeth	(May/June)
Harh	(June/July)
Sawan	(July/August)
Bhadon	(August/September)
Asu	(September/October)

In the *Nanakshahi* calendar, the year begins in *Katik* with the birthday of Guru Nanak.

Glossary

Akhand Path A non-stop reading of the Guru Granth Sahib which takes place at festivals and other special occasions.

Amrit A special mixture of sugar and water, used in Sikh ceremonies.

Amritsar A city in the Punjab, India. The Sikhs' holiest city.

Devout Very holy or religious.

Gurmukhi The script used for writing the Punjabi language.

Gurpurbs Festivals which remember key times in the lives of the Sikh Gurus.

Guru One of ten great Sikh teachers who lived between 1469 and 1708.

Gurdwara A building in which Sikhs meet to worship.

Guru Granth Sahib The holy book of the Sikhs.

Hindus Followers of the Indian religion of Hinduism.

Hinduism An ancient religion which began in India at least 4,000 years ago. It is still followed by most Indians.

Islam The religion of the Muslims. Muslims form the second biggest religious group in India. The Mughal rulers of India were Muslims.

Jore melas Joyful festivals which celebrate important events from Sikh history.

Karah parshad A sweet pudding which is shared out at the end of Sikh services and ceremonies.

Khalsa The Sikh community begun by Guru Gobind Singh in 1699. The word 'Khalsa' means pure.

Langar A meal which everyone shares at the end of a Sikh service. Also the name of the room in the Gurdwara where the meal is prepared and served.

Martyrdom The death of someone who dies for their faith. The person is called a martyr.

Muslim A follower of the religion of Islam.

Nishan Sahib The Sikh flag which flies above all Gurdwaras.

Panj Piare The first five members of the Khalsa.

Punjab The region of north-west India where Sikhism began.

Sewa The Sikh belief in helping other people as a way of serving God.

Shabads Hymns found in the Guru Granth Sahib.

Tolerance Respecting other people's beliefs and views.

Further Resources

Books

Celebrations! Baisakhi
Mandy Ross, Heinemann, 2001

Storyteller: Sikh Stories
Anita Ganeri, Evans Brothers, 2001

What do we know about Sikhism?
Beryl Dhanjal, Hodder Wayland, 1996

Introducing Religions: Sikhism
Sue Penny, Heinemann, 1997

Keystones: Sikh Gurdwara
Kanwaljit Kaur Singh, A & C Black, 1998

Festivals in World Religions
The Shap Working Party on
World Religions in Education, 1998

Beliefs and Customs: Sikh
Catherine Chambers, Watts, 1999

Websites

www.festivals.com
Information about festivals, holy days and holidays.

www.sikhs.org
Information about all aspects of Sikhism.

www.allaboutsikhs.com
More facts about Sikhs and their religion.

www.indiancultureonline.com
Details about how Sikh festivals are celebrated in India.

To find out more about Sikhism in Australia, check out **www.sikhaustralia.org** and **www.sikh.com.au**

Index

Akhand Path 12, 15, 22, 29
amrit 21, 22, 29
Amritsar 6, 8, 27, 29
Baisakhi 8, 20–23, 28
Divali 8, 26–27, 28
five Ks 21
God 6, 8, 9, 11, 16, 23, 25
Golden Temple 6, 8, 27
Gurdwara 7, 10, 12, 15, 17, 19, 22, 27
gurpurbs 7, 12, 13, 14, 15, 17, 24, 29
Guru Amar Das 8
Guru Angad Dev 8, 11
Guru Arjan Dev 8, 24–25, 26, 28
Guru Gobind Singh 8, 16–17, 18, 20, 28

Guru Granth Sahib 7, 8, 9, 12, 13, 15, 16, 17, 19, 24, 29
Guru Hargobind 8, 23, 26–27
Guru Har Krishan 8
Guru Har Rai 8
Guru Nanak 6, 8, 9, 10–11, 13, 17, 28
Guru Ram Das 8
Guru Tegh Bahadur 8, 14–15, 16, 28
Hinduism 6, 18, 26, 29
Hola Mohalla 18–19, 28
Holi 18
jore melas 7, 18, 22, 29
Kabaddi 19
karah parshad 12, 17, 29
Khalsa 8, 13, 16, 20, 21, 22, 29
khanda 23

langar 7, 12, 29
Mardana 11
martial arts 18, 19
Mool Mantar 9
names 23
New Year 20
Nihang warriors 18
Nishan Sahib 23, 29
Panj Piare 13, 17, 19, 21, 22, 29
processions 12, 13, 15, 17, 22
Punjab 6, 7, 8, 11, 18, 29
River Ravi 25
romalla 15
Sis Ganj Sahib Gurdwara 15